Revealing the Secrets of Social Media in Book Publishing

Table of Contents

1. Introduction ... 2

2. Understanding the Interplay Between Books and Social Media ... 3

    2.1. The Rise of Social Media and its Impact on the Publishing Industry ... 3

    2.2. Shaping Reader Perception through Social Media ... 4

    2.3. The Power of Hashtags and Trends ... 4

    2.4. Community Building and Engagement ... 5

3. The Importance of Building a Solid Social Media Presence ... 6

    3.1. The Emergence of Social Media as a Platform for Visibility ... 6

    3.2. Creation of Your Social Persona ... 7

    3.3. Content Is King ... 7

    3.4. Consistency Is Crucive ... 7

    3.5. Building Relationships ... 8

    3.6. Harnessing the Power of Collaboration ... 8

    3.7. Evaluating your Social Media Presence ... 8

4. Social Media Platforms: Decoding Their Unique Attributes ... 10

    4.1. Identifying the Big Five ... 10

    4.2. Striking the Right Platform Mix ... 11

    4.3. Algorithmic Nuances: Working With, Not Against ... 12

    4.4. Practical Toolkit: Profile, Content, Engagement ... 12

5. Crafting a Striking Social Media Profile for Your Book ... 14

    5.1. The Preamble: Crafting a bio ... 14

    5.2. Optimal Username and Handle Selection ... 14

    5.3. Optimal Profile Picture & Cover Photo ... 15

    5.4. Crafting Post Content ... 15

    5.5. Engagement Strategy: Respond, Interact, Repeat ... 15

    5.6. Call-to-Action: Directing Your Audience ... 16

    5.7. Consistency: The Key that Unlocks Recognition ... 16

6. Content Creation: Appealing posts for Maximum Engagement . . . 17

6.1. The Basics of Compelling Content Creation 17

6.2. The Art of Visual Storytelling 18

6.3. Writing Engaging Captions 18

6.4. Harnessing Hashtags and Emojis 19

6.5. Consistency is Key 19

7. Things to Remember: Avoiding Common Mistakes in Social
Media Marketing 21

7.1. Identifying Missteps 21

7.2. Embracing Authenticity 22

7.3. Engagement Over Numbers 22

7.4. Avoiding Common Mistakes 23

7.5. The Right Approach to Timing 23

8. Enhancing your Reach: Building and Nurturing an Online
Community 25

8.1. The Dynamics of an Online Community 25

8.2. Building the Foundations of Your Community 25

8.3. Turning Passive Followers into Active Community
Members 26

8.4. Retaining Community Members through Personalized
Interactions 26

8.5. The Power of User-Generated Content 27

8.6. Leveraging the Community for Promotional Purposes 27

8.7. Building Online Community on Different Platforms 27

8.8. Nurturing the Community: A Long-term Commitment 28

9. The Power of Influencer Marketing in Book Publishing 29

9.1. Unmasking Influencer Marketing 29

9.2. Significance of Influencer Marketing in Book Publishing . . 30

9.3. Selecting the Right Influencer 30

9.4. Crafting Collaborative Strategies 31

9.5. Measuring the Impact of Influencer Marketing 31

10. Data Analytics: Gauging Success in Social Media Campaigns . . . 33

10.1. Insights into the Power of Data Analytics 33

10.2. Vital Metrics to Track your Performance 34

10.3. Social Media Analytics Tools 34

10.4. A/B Testing: Experimenting Your Way to Success 35

10.5. The Intelligent Use of Data 35

11. Future Trends: How to Stay Ahead in Social Media Book
Marketing 37

11.1. The Era of Live Streaming 37

11.2. Augmented Reality (AR) and Virtual Reality (VR) 37

11.3. The Rise of Private Messaging and Communities 38

11.4. Artificial Intelligence and Big Data 38

11.5. The Advent of Social Commerce 39

11.6. The Power of User-Generated Content 39

Social media is not a media. The key is to listen, engage, and build relationships.

Chapter 1. Introduction

Unleash the power of hashtags, tweets, and posts! "Revealing the Secrets of Social Media in Book Publishing", an enlightening Special Report, takes you by the hand into the fascinating world of digital marketing. This enthralling guide not only makes the labyrinth of social media in book publishing much easier to navigate but also uplifts your spirits with its cheerful tone and engaging content. By unraveling the intricacies of social media, this report empowers authors, publishers, and marketers alike to harness the dynamism of social media platforms. You're just one tap away from aligning your work with today's digitally powered publishing industry. Get your hands on this report and open the doorway to a more engaging, more visible, and ultimately profitable literary venture!

Chapter 2. Understanding the Interplay Between Books and Social Media

In the high-paced, interconnected world of today, the lines separating disparate branches of knowledge and practice are becoming more blurred. Books and social media, two spheres that may have seemed unrelated not too long ago, are now comfortably intermingling, creating unique opportunities and challenges for authors, publishers, and marketers. The dance between books and social media platforms stems from a singular, cardinal fact: social media offers an unparalleled medium for engaging with millions of potential readers worldwide, amplifying one's reach far beyond traditional strategies.

2.1. The Rise of Social Media and its Impact on the Publishing Industry

The last decade has heralded an era where social media platforms have become pervasive. These digital landscapes have significantly influenced many facets of our lives, including how we choose and consume books. To understand this interplay more profoundly, we need first to examine the rise of social media platforms and their deep impact on the publishing industry.

Digital platforms like Facebook, Twitter, Instagram, and LinkedIn have emerged as vital channels for books' promotion. These platforms, each with its unique set of attributes and user demographics, are being leveraged to the hilt by publishers and authors to reach the right target audience. Bolstered by the visibility and potential virality that these platforms offer, literary works have found a new, exciting lease of life within the digital domain.

2.2. Shaping Reader Perception through Social Media

One of the most significant aspects of social media in relation to book publishing is how it directly shapes and molds reader perceptions. In traditional scenarios, a reader's primary influences were professional reviews or word-of-mouth recommendations. Social media has exponentially widened this influence sphere.

Authors and publishers can now directly interact with readers, sparking engaging discussions, sharing insights into the creative process, and building anticipation with sneak peeks and teasers. Readers, in turn, can voice their opinions, write reviews, and recommend books within their network, augmenting the book's visibility organically.

The immediate, two-way communication facilitated by social platforms has consequently created a more dynamic and participatory relationship between authors, publishers, and readers, helping shape a more inclusive and democratic literary landscape.

2.3. The Power of Hashtags and Trends

A distinctive feature of social media platforms is the use of hashtags and their ability to set trends. Hashtags essentially act as a categorization feature, allowing individuals to follow specific topics of interest, conversations, and trends. They can prove instrumental in promoting a book, creating a buzz around it, or even setting up an entire community powered by passionate discussions about the book.

For example, a unique hashtag related to a book or author can be propagated across social networks to generate awareness and interest. As more people join the conversation using this hashtag, it could potentially emerge as a trend. Publishers and authors can leverage this viral feature to cast a wider net over potential audience pools, significantly amplifying the book's reach and impact.

2.4. Community Building and Engagement

In essence, social media platforms are built around the idea of community. They're spaces where like-minded individuals can come together, share thoughts, and engage in enriching discussions. This aspect resonates magnificently well with the world of books, given how they inherently foster deep thought, dialogue, and introspection.

Authors can build a community around their books, fostering an environment where readers can discuss plot points, themes, and character arcs. Such spaces can transform followers into loyal readers, creating a consistent, engaged reader base for current and future works. Publishers, too, can benefit immensely from this feature, forming communities around genres, authors, or their brand, thereby generating a network of eager readers awaiting their next release.

In conclusion, the interplay between social media and books is undeniably profound, reshaping the way books are marketed and consumed. By understanding the intrinsic ties between these entities, authors, publishers, and marketers can harness the power of digital platforms, potentially revolutionizing their reach and influence within the literary universe. This in-depth exploration serves as the springboard into deeper topics addressed in subsequent chapters, each shedding light on the multi-faceted role of social media in book publishing.

Chapter 3. The Importance of Building a Solid Social Media Presence

In the vast interconnected ocean that is the modern digital landscape, the importance of constructing a robust presence on social media cannot be overstated. Like a beacon on the shore, guiding ships to safe harbor, a strong social media presence helps readers navigate the overwhelming quantity of content available today, beckoning them towards your books.

3.1. The Emergence of Social Media as a Platform for Visibility

Modern society lives and breathes social media in all its forms: the snappy, ephemeral Tweets, the vibrant and colorful posts on Instagram, the shared-interest communities on Facebook. No wonder publishing houses and authors gravitate towards these platforms—to not leverage them would be to ignore a powerful tool at their disposal.

Building a strong social media presence is pivotal to integrating oneself into the digital landscape. Engagement levels on these platforms have steadily risen over the years, turning them into bustling hubs of interaction where potential readers gather, discuss and discover new books. In fact, social media's ubiquity has made it a significant discovery platform, often democratizing the book discovery process which traditionally relied heavily on large publishing houses.

3.2. Creation of Your Social Persona

The core of social media is interaction, and interaction hinges on personality. Therefore, the first step is to contemplate about your social persona. Identify how you wish to represent yourself, your books, and your brand. Careful attention needs to be paid while crafting your online identity—your tone of voice, style of communication, and type of content all contribute to this persona. Being able to resonate with your target audience is crucial, so maintain an authentic, relatable persona that aligns with your brand values.

3.3. Content Is King

The mantra for successful social media presence undeniably is: Content is King. Effective utilization of hashtags, visuals, and organic posts are key to creating engaging content. Moreover, the content you share should not only promote your books, it must provide value to your readers. Ideally, it should stir emotions, spark conversations, and encourage sharing. Timely and relevant content, coupled with a proper understanding of algorithmic behavior specific to each platform, can significantly amplify your visibility and reach.

3.4. Consistency Is Crucive

Developing a robust social media presence doesn't happen overnight; it's a long-term endeavor that demands consistency. Consistency goes beyond regularly publishing content—it extends to maintaining a consistent tone, style, and messaging across your posts and interactions, reinforcing your brand identity.

3.5. Building Relationships

Now comes the human part of social media—the building and nurturing of relationships. Engage with your audience, respond to their comments, partake in conversations, and instigate discussions. Encouraging interaction not only allows you to better understand your audience but also fosters a sense of community around your work, turning casual followers into ardent supporters.

3.6. Harnessing the Power of Collaboration

Collaborations and partnerships with other authors, influencers, or literary platforms can augment your online presence. Such collaborations, whether they involve guest posts, joint ventures, or promotional exchanges, can introduce you to new audiences, enhancing your visibility and appeal.

3.7. Evaluating your Social Media Presence

Finally, continual evaluation and improvement are vital. Use analytics and feedback to measure the effectiveness of your strategies, adapting and evolving your practices based on these insights.

Building a robust social media presence might seem like an arduous task, but by breaking it down into these steps—defining and maintaining a consistent social persona, curating engaging and valuable content, fostering relationships through engagement, leveraging collaborations, and conducting regular evaluations—you will set the stage for a successful relationship with your readers in the digital world.

Mastering the art and science of social media allows you to connect with your readers in a deeply personal way, bringing visibility to your work and fostering a community of loyal readers who are more than just spectators—they are active participants in your journey. A solid social media presence not only gives your book the platform it deserves but also redefines the author-reader relationship in the 21st century, making it more engaging, interactive, and personal.

Chapter 4. Social Media Platforms: Decoding Their Unique Attributes

In the vast ecosystem of social media sites, each platform emerges with unique characteristics and strengths, catering to different demographic groups and goals. In this space, understanding the distinctive undertones and capabilities of the specific platforms is essential in designing effective book marketing campaigns.

4.1. Identifying the Big Five

A key step in forming your social media strategy involves understanding the "Big Five" platforms—Facebook, Twitter, LinkedIn, Instagram, and YouTube. These titan platforms of social media provide the greatest reach and impact and have the most diverse user bases.

Facebook, the reigning champion of social platforms, has over 2.8 billion monthly active users. Facebook is beloved for its global reach and versatility, accommodating various forms of content such as text-based posts, photos, as well as videos. It also features business-oriented tools, including paid ads, Facebook pages, and groups that facilitate interaction among users with common interests.

Twitter, with its 330 million active users, hosts an expansive dialogue in succinct, rapid-fire tweets that iterate and soar at breathtaking speed. Key for brevity and immediacy, Twitter is particularly helpful in spreading your message quickly, join trending conversations and engage with followers in real-time.

LinkedIn, the professional networking platform, presents a more sophisticated avenue for purposeful B2B interactions and career networking. With its 766 million users, LinkedIn cautions thoughtfulness and professionality in communication.

Instagram, with its focus on visual content which includes images and short videos, is a remarkable platform for showcasing your book in a visually appealing manner to its over 1 billion users. Its appeal lies in visual storytelling through beautiful cover photos, behind-the-scenes glimpses, and engaging quote designs.

YouTube, the second largest search engine after Google, is the leading platform for video content. With more than 2 billion logged-in monthly users, it offers a unique space for authors to share their work through readings, book trailers, author interviews, and more.

4.2. Striking the Right Platform Mix

Once you've grasped the nature and potential of these platforms, the next step is determining where you should establish your presence. The right blend of platforms for your strategy will depend upon your book's target demographics, as different platforms attract different age groups, and interests. Remember, the goal is not to be present everywhere but to be effective where you are present.

For instance, if your book is targeted towards a younger readership, visual-heavy platforms like Instagram and TikTok cater to this demographic exceptionally well. Conversely, if your work caters to a professional audience, LinkedIn might be the appropriate channel to focus your efforts.

Moreover, consider the characteristics of your book. Is the narrative visually appealing and design-centric? Then Instagram could be a perfect fit. Does your book touch on current affairs or news topics? In this case, the real-time nature of Twitter can be used effectively.

4.3. Algorithmic Nuances: Working With, Not Against

Different social media platforms employ different algorithms to decide what content gets seen by which users. Familiarity with these specifics allows you to work with the algorithm, not against it, increasing your chances of reaching the widest possible audience.

For example, Facebook's algorithm greatly favors content that fosters meaningful interactions. Therefore, creating engaging content that encourages comments, shares, and reactions from users will gain much more visibility.

Instagram's algorithm, on the other hand, is heavily influenced by the popularity of the posts, timeliness, and the relationship between the uploader and the user.

Twitter provides the most real-time content amongst all platforms but has its own set of algorithmic factors. It takes into account the recency of the tweet, relevance to the user, and the engagement it receives.

LinkedIn prioritizes relevancy, focusing heavily on content that is related to a user's industry or profession. YouTube utilizes watch time, relevance, and viewer engagement in its algorithm.

4.4. Practical Toolkit: Profile, Content, Engagement

A practical toolkit is essential to use social media platforms effectively. Your profile should be well-crafted, clear, and compelling, aimed at attracting and retaining followers. Your content should consistently resonate with your target audience, fostering a relationship that extends beyond the sale of a single book.

Engagement is equally vital. Reply to comments, like and share posts, follow back, and start conversations. Engagement will not only make your followers feel valued but also increase your visibility across the platforms.

Through understanding, selecting, and utilizing the unique attributes of different social media platforms, you can effectively wield these tools to amplify your book's presence in the crowded digital marketplace. Your efforts will contribute significantly to the visibility and success of your book, painting a robust and vibrant social media canvas for your literary endeavors.

Chapter 5. Crafting a Striking Social Media Profile for Your Book

A commanding presence on social media doesn't magically happen; it is crafted strategically and thoughtfully. To be successful in digital marketing for book publishing, an attractive and compelling social media profile is essential. From choosing a catchy username to employing a visually appealing theme, how effectively you present your book on social media can dramatically enhance its visibility and impact. This chapter delves into the art and science of crafting a social media profile that can draw in readers and generate engagement.

5.1. The Preamble: Crafting a bio

First impressions last, which is why your bio should be an accurate yet enticing encapsulation of your book. It should tell your prospective readers who you are, what you do, and what to expect from your book. The bio needs to be succinct but stimulating enough to arouse interest. Depending on the platform, character limits may constrain your writing. For example, Twitter allows a maximum of 160 characters. Despite the limitations, you could experiment with short sentences, emotive language, emojis, or even hashtags. Remember to include your book's website link and other relevant contact info, if possible.

5.2. Optimal Username and Handle Selection

Selecting an effective username and handle is next. Your username must be unique, easy to remember, and expressive of your book's essence. Handles can typically be changed but remember that consistency across platforms aids in brand recognition. If an exact match is not available, use variations that still tie closely to your book.

5.3. Optimal Profile Picture & Cover Photo

Your profile picture and cover photo are the visual "bookcovers" of your social media pages. The priority should always be to use high-quality, professional and thematically relevant images that visually articulate your book's concept or theme. A well-designed book cover or an author's persona often work well. By contrast, the cover photo offers a larger canvas to play with. This space can be used to highlight a quote from the book, display a collage of art related to the book, or even showcase reader testimonials.

5.4. Crafting Post Content

With the profile basics covered, the next step focuses on crafting the content of your posts. This demands a mix of creativity, authenticity, and relevance. Strive to strike a balance between promotional posts and engaging content such as book excerpts, author interviews, behind-the-scenes snippets, reader reviews, interactive quizzes or polls, giveaways, etc. Always remember, being authentic and engaging is key to building rapport and trust with your audience.

5.5. Engagement Strategy: Respond, Interact, Repeat

A major part of creating a striking social media profile is your engagement strategy. Regularly responding to comments, participating in discussions, and acknowledging shares or retweets can create a ripple effect of engagement. Another key aspect of this strategy is offering value to your followers through educational or informative content, or simply by sharing content with a touch of your personal flair.

5.6. Call-to-Action: Directing Your Audience

A Call-to-Action (CTA) is a potent tool for turning passive onlookers into engaged readers and potential book buyers. Clearly state what you would like followers to do after they read your post; this could be visiting your website, signing up for an event, or buying your book.

5.7. Consistency: The Key that Unlocks Recognition

Consistency across all aspects of your social media profile is indispensable. Your visuals, tone, and posting schedule should align and stay consistent so followers always know what to expect. This facilitates better brand recognition and trust among your audience.

Your digital presence on social media is a powerful extension of your book and, ultimately, your brand. Craft it thoughtfully to make a significant and lasting impression. This chapter reveals that creating a striking social media profile is not only about aesthetic appeal but also about forming connections, establishing your brand, and adding value to your audience. It's an ongoing process that requires creativity, attention to detail, and adaptability. With every post, interaction, and decision, you are one step closer to shaping your robust social media image and amplifying your book's reach.

Chapter 6. Content Creation: Appealing posts for Maximum Engagement

Creating engaging posts is the bedrock upon which successful social media marketing campaigns are built. It is with these posts that you can capture the attention of your audience, converting casual readers into committed followers and buyers. Whether you're announcing a new book release, sharing a thought-provoking excerpt or merely promoting a sale, how you present your message matters. An understanding of compelling content creation is key to making social media work for your book.

6.1. The Basics of Compelling Content Creation

Content is considered the lifeblood of social media, given its power to captivate, engage, and convince the audience. Unlike a traditional billboard that screams promotions and discounts, the nature of social media content is sensitive, requiring it to be appealing rather than purely promotional.

The first step in creating engaging posts is to know your audience. For whom are you creating content? It would help to identify common characteristics of your target audience: their common age range, interests, and the typical platforms they frequent. Knowing your audience not only places you in a position to understand what they might enjoy but also empowers you to create content that they can connect with on a deeper level.

Next, consider your book's genre and tone. The content you create needs to match these elements to create a sense of uniformity which your audience can familiarize themselves with. For example, if your book is a light-hearted romance, using humor and romantic quotes in your posts could resonate with your audience. On the flip side, if you're promoting a deep, thought-provoking novel, incorporating philosophic quotes or questions in your posts could be a way to engage your followers.

6.2. The Art of Visual Storytelling

While the written word is important in content creation, the contemporary statutes of social media engagement uphold the reign of visual storytelling. On platforms where users scroll quickly, attention spans are at their shortest. As such, compelling visuals like infographics, videos, pictures, memes, or animated gifs can break through the scrolling monotony and get users to pause and engage with your content.

Using visually appealing book covers, behind-the-scenes images, author interviews, or storyboards can portray the personality of your book, which can spark the interest of potential readers. Additionally, they can keep your existing readers engaged and excited for your future publication.

Furthermore, remember that different platforms may require different formats. For instance, Instagram is keener on vertical images, while Twitter and Facebook lean towards horizontal ones. Thus, every visual element in your content strategy should align with each platform's preferences for maximum impact.

6.3. Writing Engaging Captions

Even if your image is worth a thousand words, meticulously crafted captions add depth to your posts and can greatly enhance their engagement potential. In crafting captions, your aim should be to offer value, provoke thought, or stir emotions.

Captions can be a mix of behind-the-scenes information, related quotes, questions that stimulate dialogue, or interesting snippets from your book's content. Always aim for authenticity and relevance. Consider your audience's preferences over catchy phrases that may seem out of place.

6.4. Harnessing Hashtags and Emojis

Hashtags and emojis might seem small elements, but they can significantly contribute to the success of your posts. Hashtags make your content discoverable, ultimately increasing your visibility on social platforms. They can relate to your book, writing process, the genre, or even trending topics that relate to your story or subject matter.

Emojis allow you to convey emotions and ideas that might be challenging to highlight with words. They also help to soften your language, making your posts more approachable and relatable.

6.5. Consistency is Key

Consistency is one of the most critical attributes that can define the success of your content creation and ultimately, your overall social media marketing. Regularly sharing high-quality posts not only keeps your audience engaged but also accentuates your presence on social media, increasing your visibility on respective platforms.

Remember, the creation of appealing posts for maximum engagement is but one part of a larger social media strategy. Each aspect of your digital marketing campaign should seamlessly integrate with others for harmony in your communication, thus propelling your book publishing endeavors on social media platforms. Through such relentless effort and consistent attention to detail, you can create an echo in the vast digital landscape that is social media, ultimately increasing your audience engagement, book visibility, and sales.

Chapter 7. Things to Remember: Avoiding Common Mistakes in Social Media Marketing

In the intoxicating swirl of social media marketing, it is all too easy for authors, publishers, and marketing pros to get lost and make unnecessary errors that could stymie their book's potential success. By identifying and understanding such pitfalls, you can turn the tide and make your online presence count. Explore how to avoid common mistakes in your social media marketing strategy and set your books up for sparkling results.

7.1. Identifying Missteps

Social media marketing isn't merely about being visible online. It's an intricate process that requires a thorough understanding of your audience, the platform you're using, and the content you're sharing. The first pitfall trap is a failure to identify with all these aspects. Ignoring even one could lead to diminished reach and impact.

1. Understanding Your Audience: Rule number one is knowing who your audience is. A wrong assessment here could mean that your message resonates with the wrong crowd, yielding unimpressive results. Focus on understanding their demographics, interests, and online behaviors.

2. Using the Right Platform: Equally pivotal is picking the appropriate platform. A mistake here could signify squandering resources on an audience that is not interested in your book's genre or subject matter. Carefully evaluate the unique attributes of each platform and the kind of audience they cater to.

3. Crafting Engaging Content: Even if the previous two points are on the mark, lackluster content can ruin your chances of success. Ensure that your posts are entertaining, educational, and engaging to your targeted audience.

7.2. Embracing Authenticity

One can't emphasize enough the importance of authenticity in social media marketing. Readers and potential buyers appreciate genuineness. Inauthentic posts or feeds can make followers disconnect and eventually drift away. So, remember:

- Be True to Yourself and Your Book: Keep your posts authentic and aligned with your persona and your book's theme. Inconsistencies can dilute your brand and put off potential readers.

- Spontaneity and Consistency: While planning and scheduling posts is important, maintaining some spontaneity is crucial as well. A consistent but robotic feed lacking genuine interaction does little in cementing relationships with followers.

7.3. Engagement Over Numbers

It is easy to get swept by the mania of vanity metrics, where high follower count may seem to equate higher reach. While numbers matter, what really creates an impact is engagement and interaction.

- Understanding Metrics: Instead of relying solely on follower count, use inbuilt analytical tools to delve deeper into metrics like engagement rate, click-through rate, etc.

- Engage, Don't Just Post: Make your social media presence interactive. Respond to comments, encourage conversations, and let your followers know you value their inputs.

7.4. Avoiding Common Mistakes

We have all experienced a social media faux pas. Lost followers, low engagement, or the dreaded trolls can be discouraging. Avoid these common mistakes:

- Over-Promotion: Avoid turning your social media profile into a sales page. Your followers are looking for entertainment and interaction, not perpetual sales pitches.

- Neglecting Negative Feedback: It's unwise to ignore negative feedback. Instead, acknowledge it with politeness, learn from it, and make necessary changes.

- Inconsistency: Inconsistent posting can confuse your audience and stunt your growth. Strike a balance between being spontaneous and having a frequent posting schedule.

7.5. The Right Approach to Timing

The time you post matters. A lack of understanding about your followers' online activity can result in your content being lost in the feed.

- Know Your Timing: Use analytics tools to understand when most of your followers are active and schedule your posts accordingly.

- Don't Flood, Space Out: Avoid dumping all your posts at once. Space them out evenly to enhance visibility and engagement.

In conclusion, circumventing common mistakes in social media marketing isn't insuperable. It necessitates keen understanding, sincere effort, and patience. By keeping these pointers in mind, you can make the most of your social media venture, connecting effectively with your audience and boosting your book's success. Remember, social media marketing for books is not about winning a race. It's about building a community that trusts, appreciates, and lauds your work.

Chapter 8. Enhancing your Reach: Building and Nurturing an Online Community

Mastering the realm of social media involves more than just making occasional posts on Twitter or sporadically tossing pictures on Instagram. To truly leverage social media for your book marketing needs, you must understand and embrace one key strategy: building and nurturing an online community. It will not only broaden your reach but also turn casual observers into fervent advocates of your book.

8.1. The Dynamics of an Online Community

An online community, in essence, is a circle of individuals who share a common interest and are bonded through the wonders of digital space. There are several noteworthy characteristics of these communities: they are centered around one main focus (in this instance, your book), they are organically constructed, and most importantly, they offer an ongoing and highly interactive experience. Now, let's embark on the process of building and nurturing these valuable communities.

8.2. Building the Foundations of Your Community

To create an effective online community around your book, it would be best to begin with a thorough analysis of your target audience.

Determine the age range, gender, profession, hobbies, preferences, and other demographics of your ideal readers. Armed with this understanding, you can begin crafting content that caters specifically to your audience - this ideation is the core around which your community will coalesce. Begin the community-construction process by inviting your established social media followers to join a dedicated space—this can be a forum, social media group, or a mailing list.

8.3. Turning Passive Followers into Active Community Members

The next step is the transformation of passive followers into active community members. Foster an environment where followers feel encouraged to share their opinions, feedback, ask questions, and engage in lively discussion. This can be achieved through various engagement strategies. For example, organize Q&A sessions, conduct polls or quizzes related to your book, or launch a contest with attractive rewards. This gamification strategy will likely intrigue followers and incite proactive participation, thereby strengthening the community bond.

8.4. Retaining Community Members through Personalized Interactions

Once you've succeeded in creating an engaging environment, prioritize retaining readers by highlighting the advantages of being a part of your community. Engage further with them by responding candidly to their comments or posing open-ended questions that prompt debates. Personalized interactions give community members the feeling of being valued and understood, hence enhancing the possibility of them remaining loyal to your brand.

8.5. The Power of User-Generated Content

User-generated content (UGC) is a powerful tool to boost your community's growth. Encourage members to share their experiences related to your book – this may include reviews, pictures or videos of them reading your book, fan art, or personal takeaways. Not only does this stimulate conversation within the community, but it also serves as a means of outward promotion when other non-community members see this content.

8.6. Leveraging the Community for Promotional Purposes

While it is crucial to not over-commercialize your community space, it can certainly be utilized for promotional purposes. Use your community to announce your latest news, like book launches or author meets. You can also use it as a testing ground for new book ideas by seeking community feedback. Turning your community into a direct marketing channel, however, risks alienating members, so use this sparingly and always ensure that your promotional activities provide value to your followers.

8.7. Building Online Community on Different Platforms

Building your community across different platforms expands your reach and presence. Yet the rules of engagement differ from one platform to another. For Twitter, engaging with hashtags related to your book genre and creating Twitter chats can be beneficial. Using Facebook, organize contests, live Q&A sessions, and create groups dedicated to your book. Instagram can leverage behind-the-scenes content, book excerpts, quotes, or visually appealing book designs. For Goodreads, engage with your readers via polls, quizzes, and exclusive author interviews and encourage them to add your book to their reading lists and write reviews.

8.8. Nurturing the Community: A Long-term Commitment

Building a thriving online community is not a one-off task. It requires continuous effort and investment (in terms of time and creativity). Post consistently, engage regularly, keep up with the latest trends, and always elicit feedback from your community members. Over time, you will not only see a blossoming digital community but also experience the rewards in the form of increased book exposure, better feedback, and enhanced reader loyalty.

In summary, creating and nurturing a vibrant online community is a rewarding process that requires a careful blend of analysis, interaction, encouragement, and ongoing engagement. By doing so, you can harness the power of collective excitement about your book, turning readers from casual fans into fervent advocates of your work.

Chapter 9. The Power of Influencer Marketing in Book Publishing

In the domain of digital marketing, influencer marketing stands out as a burgeoning strategy with untapped potential. Particularly in book publishing, the role of influencers is rapidly making a headway, bridging the gap between authors, their work, and their prospective readers. The subsequent segments delve extensively into this area, elucidating the niche aspects related to influencer marketing in book publishing.

9.1. Unmasking Influencer Marketing

In the most simplistic terms, influencer marketing is a strategy that incorporates individuals with substantial followings on social media platforms into a company's or individual's marketing campaigns. This strategy's fundamental assumption is that these influencers have garnered enough trust and credibility among their followers that their recommendations and endorsements will drive consumer behavior, including book purchases.

As we venture into the realm of book publishing, influencers could include famous authors, book critics, reviewers, popular book bloggers, booktubers, and even celebrities known for their love of reading. An influencer's endorsement of a book can significantly boost sales, generate buzz, and expand the author's reach into uncharted reader circles.

9.2. Significance of Influencer Marketing in Book Publishing

At the heart of influencer marketing is the power of word-of-mouth. A personal recommendation from a trusted source remains unequivocally one of the strongest marketing tools, even in this digital era. This aspect is of prime importance in the publishing industry. When an influencer gives a positive review or endorsement, it not only raises awareness but also enhances the book's credibility. This, in turn, can propel a crucial spike in book sales and reader engagement.

Along with organic reach, influencer marketing also engages niche audiences effectively. Influencers in the literary world have curated communities with particular reading interests. Thus, a YA fantasy author could sync with a blogger who specializes in YA fantasy literature, ensuring their work reaches the right audience.

9.3. Selecting the Right Influencer

Influencer marketing is a nuanced strategy that necessitates identifying and collaborating with the right influencers. You must first understand who converses with your target demographic and holds an authoritative voice in your exact genre or industry. Evaluate the influencer's followers, the engagement rate, and the credibility they hold in their community.

Always remember, the influencer's follower count is often misleading. A niche influencer with fewer followers might prove more beneficial if their audience is genuinely interested and engaged in their content. It's the quality of followers, not the quantity, that matters the most.

9.4. Crafting Collaborative Strategies

After identifying potential influencers, it is crucial to forge symbiotic relationships with them. Better cooperation can yield more authentic endorsements, thereby improving the campaign's overall performance.

It is noteworthy that influencers tend to work best when given creative freedom. Instead of dictating the endorsement's format or message, allow the influencer to represent your book in a fashion that resonates with their audience.

Strategies for collaboration can involve free book copies, exclusive author interviews, book launch event invitations, among others. These help the influencer to frame a well-informed view, and the endorsement becomes a genuine reflection of their opinion.

9.5. Measuring the Impact of Influencer Marketing

Paralleling any marketing tactic, evaluating the effectiveness of an influencer campaign is paramount. Translating social media activity into book sales can be complex, but it remains an essential task. Tools for such assessments can range from discount codes and affiliate marketing links used by the influencer to more intricate tools like web analytics and data analysis software.

Influencer marketing, like social media itself, is a dynamic, ever-evolving field. As the landscape changes, new influencers emerge, and fresh approaches to collaboration and campaign design are necessitated. The key, then, lies in adaptation and continued learning. With its unique ability to engage and resonate with readers, the power of influencer marketing in publishing cannot be underestimated. With the careful selection of influencers, thoughtful collaboration, and measured results, influencer marketing strategies can undeniably level up the success of your book on social media platforms.

Chapter 10. Data Analytics: Gauging Success in Social Media Campaigns

In the realm of social media marketing, data analytics plays a crucial, almost prophetic role. It enables you to peer into the success, or lack thereof, of your campaigns, offering a window into how your audience is engaging with your content. More importantly, it provides a roadmap for tweaking your content strategy to optimise engagement and amplify your book's visibility.

10.1. Insights into the Power of Data Analytics

Data Analytics is like the compass guiding a ship in the uncharted waters of the social media oceans. It revolves around collecting, analyzing, and interpreting data, with a view to understanding patterns of user interactions. A comprehensive study of data can provide valuable insights into audience behavior, thereby enabling the formation of a coherent and impact-driven social media strategy.

Consider data analytics as your ultimate handy tool to decipher the response of your readers and their engagement with your posts. Not only does it help you understand who your audience is—geography, demographics, and interests—it also provides valuable insights into the kind of posts that resonate with them, and the timing that leads to maximum interactions.

10.2. Vital Metrics to Track your Performance

Understanding which metrics to track is pivotal to gauge the success of your social media campaigns. Let's delve into the key performance indicators (KPIs) that bear the most significance in data analytics.

1. Reach: This defines the number of unique users who viewed your content. By tracking reach, you can effectively measure the breadth of your campaign, providing you a yardstick to ascertain whether your messages are permeating beyond your immediate followers.

2. Impressions: An impression refers to the total times your content was displayed on someone's social media feed, regardless of engagement. Impressions help you glean the total potential visibility of your content.

3. Engagement: This involves any interaction a user has with your content — likes, comments, shares, retweets, clicks, and more. This reflects how your content strikes a chord with the audience, leading them to respond or participate.

4. Click-through Rate (CTR): This metric is the ratio of users who click on a specific link/the total number of users who view the content. CTR offers insights into how effectively your content encourages users to take the desired action.

5. Conversion Rate: This metric underlines the percentage of users who completed a desired action or goal through your social media content. This could be purchasing your book, subscribing to your newsletter, or downloading a sample chapter.

10.3. Social Media Analytics Tools

Your mission to collect, interpret, and react to social media data will be incomplete without the use of competent analytics tools. These tools equip you with crucial insights into the performance of your campaigns, helping adjust your strategies accordingly.

1. Facebook Insights and Instagram Insights: These native analytical tools come with the platforms and provide detailed statistics about your posts' reach, impressions, engagement, demographics of followers, and optimal posting times, among others.

2. Google Analytics: This tool is paramount when it comes to tracking conversion rates, especially when they direct users to your website or a specific landing page.

3. Hootsuite Analytics: Hootsuite isn't only a social media scheduling tool but also boasts an impressive analytics feature. It aggregates data from various platforms, helping you measure and compare the performance across platforms.

4. Sprout Social: This platform offers comprehensive data analytics, providing user-friendly reports that you can customize to suit your requirements.

10.4. A/B Testing: Experimenting Your Way to Success

Running a successful social media campaign is largely a game of intelligent, data-driven experimentation. A/B testing is a core part of this. It entails creating two versions of a piece of content, with slight variability in an element, and observing which version elicits greater engagement. Data thus collected can help improve future content and optimize engagement.

10.5. The Intelligent Use of Data

The diligent and intelligent use of data analytics can guide the route to your success in social media marketing. By scrutinizing the patterns unveiled by analytics, you can design your campaigns to appeal more effectively to your audience, understand what does and does not work, and continually adapt to maximize your reach and engagement. After all, knowledge is power - and in social media marketing for book publishing, the power lies in understanding the secrets revealed by data analytics. As you continue to delve deeper into this field, you will become more adept at navigating the circuitous routes of social media. Always remember, every tweet, every post, every hashtag, and most importantly, every interaction counts and should be studied for higher chances of success.

Chapter 11. Future Trends: How to Stay Ahead in Social Media Book Marketing

The blinding pace of evolution in the social media landscape necessitates staying informed about both, the current trends and future trajectories. It is important to anticipate, comprehend, and incorporate these trends in your social media strategies to keep your book marketing campaigns relevant, engaging, and effective. This chapter will take you on an exploratory journey into the foreseeable future of social media in book marketing.

11.1. The Era of Live Streaming

Live streaming is steadily gaining traction in the social media universe. Platforms like Facebook, Instagram and LinkedIn have all integrated this exciting capability into their features, allowing users to share real-time videos with their followers. In the context of book marketing, this technology holds a plethora of possibilities. Authors can hold live readings, reveal behind-the-scenes insights about their writing process, or even conduct virtual book launches. This real-time interaction can forge a deeper connection with the readers, fostering a more engaged and loyal fan base.

11.2. Augmented Reality (AR) and Virtual Reality (VR)

The next monumental shift in social media marketing might well come from the widespread adoption of AR and VR technologies. Social media platforms like Snapchat and Instagram already offer AR filters that significantly boost user engagement. In future, book marketers could leverage AR to offer immersive book trailers, virtual book tours or even allow potential readers to experience segments of the book in a gamified fashion. VR can elevate these experiences further by enabling readers to plunge into a full-fledged immersive experience of the book's world.

11.3. The Rise of Private Messaging and Communities

Social media users are increasingly valuing privacy, leading to the rise of private messaging and online communities. This trend offers a new avenue for book marketers – creating closed communities or groups around their books or genres. Such spaces provide bespoke and tailored content to the members, fostering a sense of belongingness and deeper engagement. WhatsApp, Facebook Groups, and LinkedIn Groups are rapidly becoming crucial channels for cultivating and nurturing such communities.

11.4. Artificial Intelligence and Big Data

Artificial Intelligence (AI) coupled with big data is poised to revolutionize how marketers understand and target their audience. By processing vast amounts of data, AI can make intelligent predictions about consumer behavior. In the realm of book marketing, this could mean personalized recommendations, understanding reader sentiments, optimizing post timings, and so much more. By embracing AI, book marketers can significantly enhance their precision and efficiency.

11.5. The Advent of Social Commerce

Social Commerce, the blending of social media and e-commerce, is burgeoning. The convergence of the consumption journey, from discovery to purchase, on a single platform greatly streamlines the user experience. Future book marketers could leverage this to allow potential readers to buy a book directly from their social media feeds, reducing drop-offs and boosting sales.

11.6. The Power of User-Generated Content

User-generated content (UGC) is a powerful tool that can amplify credibility and authenticity. Encouraging readers to share their reviews, opinions, or creative outputs pertaining to your book can not only drive engagement but also serve as testimonials that boost your book's trustworthiness. As social media evolves, UGC will remain a strong pillar of effective book marketing.

Taking all these trends into account, it becomes evident that the future of social media book marketing is not merely about having an online presence but rather weaving a holistic and immersive narrative using cutting-edge technologies and personalized content. By understanding and adapting to these trends, book marketers can ensure that their social media strategies remain effective, engaging, and capable of winning the continuous competition for reader attention.